Martial Arts

Eamonn O'Farrell

Contents

What is Martial Arts?

Martial arts is a kind of sport.
Lots of people learn martial arts.
It is fun to try.

Martial arts is hard work.
It takes a long time to be good at martial arts.

Uniform

This is a martial arts **uniform**. It is a white uniform with a belt. The colour of the belt shows how good you are.

When you begin to learn martial arts, you have a white belt.

beginner

expert

Respect

Respect is important in martial arts.
A bow is a way to show respect.
You bow to your teacher and other students.

Standing

There are many ways to stand in martial arts. The way you stand is called a **stance**.

Ready stance

Forward stance

Horseriding stance

The eyes look straight ahead.

One fist is forward.

One fist is at the side.

The legs are bent.

Tiger stance

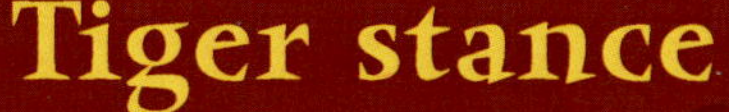

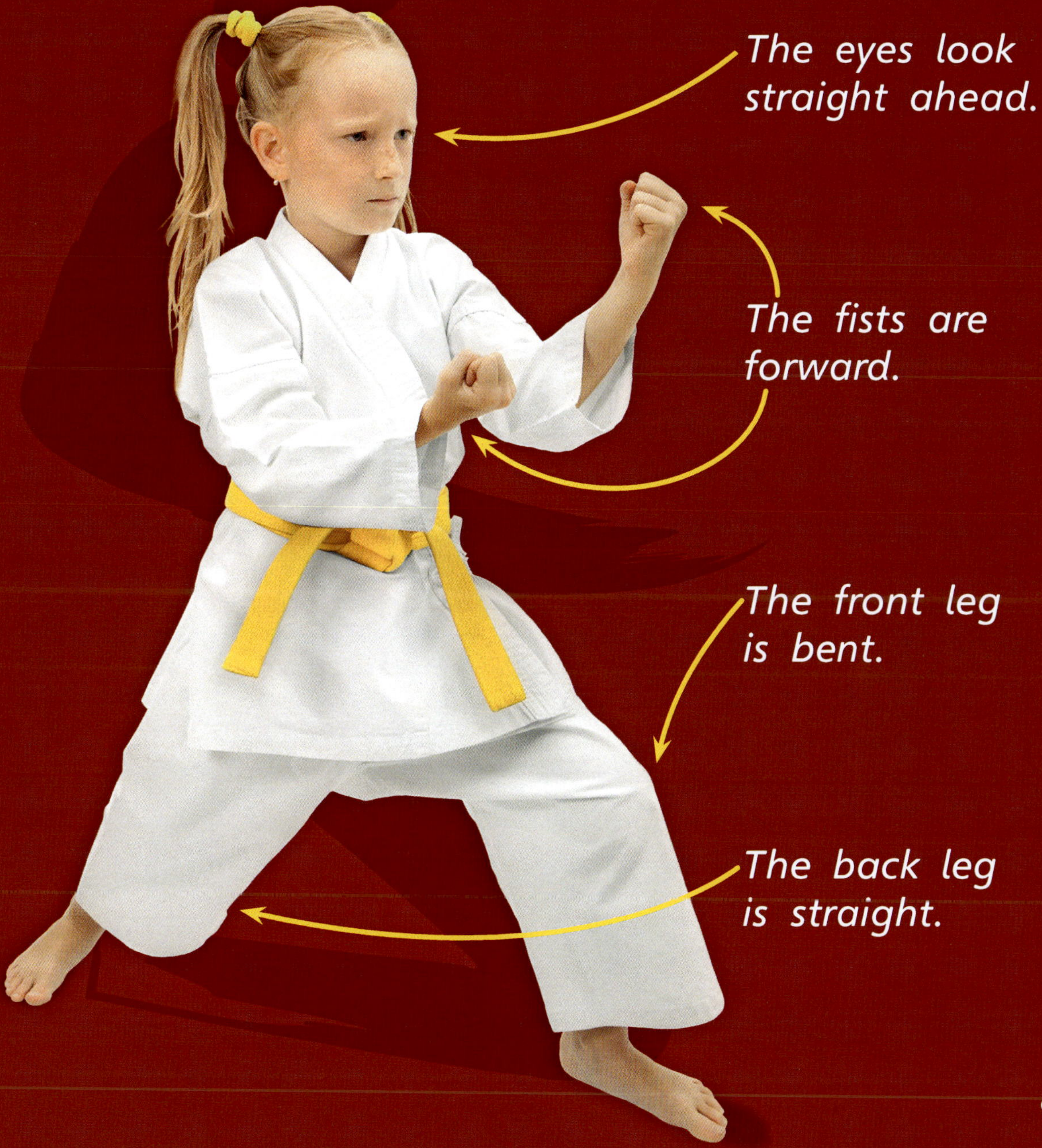
The eyes look straight ahead.
The fists are forward.
The front leg is bent.
The back leg is straight.

Punching

A punch is a type of hit in martial arts. You punch with your fist shut.

The wrist is straight.

The fingers are folded.

The thumb is outside the fingers.

The elbow is close to the body.

You can also learn to block a punch.

Kicking

A kick is a kind of hit in martial arts. There are many kinds of kicks.

The arms are up.

The knees are bent.

The heel is forward.

The leg is up high.

Side kick

Practising

When you learn martial arts, you do it with another person.

You put all your moves together – standing, punching and kicking.

If you learn martial arts for a long time, you might be able to do this!

Glossary

martial arts	types of fighting and self-defence
respect	showing care for other people and treating them well
stance	the way you hold your body while standing
uniform	clothing worn by members of a group